HOME
OFFICES

Spaces for working @ home

HOME OFFICES

Spaces for working @ home

LOFT

Editorial Coordination: Cristina Paredes
Texts: Cristian Campos
Translation: Bridget Vranckx
Art Director: Mireia Casanovas Soley
Layout and Graphic Design:
TRAMA, Estudi Gràfic
www.tramaestudi.com

Editorial project:

2008 © **LOFT Publications**
Via Laietana 32, 4º Of. 92
08003 Barcelona, Spain
Tel.: +34 932 688 088
Fax: +34 932 687 073
loft@loftpublications.com
www.loftpublications.com

ISBN: 978-84-95832-71-9

Printed in China

8

10

40

78

100

120

152

190

Our work habits are changing. More and more people, especially liberal professionals and those who have creative occupations, choose to work away from the crammed and impersonal offices of their companies. The alternative, the office at home, has slowly become the favored solution for those who cannot practice their profession within rigid hierarchical structures or for those who do not depend on a strictly centralized flow of information. The consolidation of the internet and new technologies has made it possible to turn something that was a dream only a few years ago into a normal routine for millions of people around the world.

HOME OFFICES also has its drawbacks, though, some serious enough for those thinking about taking the plunge to consider getting the professional help of an interior designer. And, we are not only talking about the discipline needed to organize our professional diary without the presence of a boss setting deadlines and timetables.

Interior designers, and even friends who have taken the step before us, can be an invaluable source of help, advice and experience, though at the end of the day, we are the ones who decide how we want our work space to be, where we want to put things, how we want it to work, where we want to store work materials, how we illuminate the space and how we decorate it so that it adapts to our tastes and not to a supposedly functional yet impersonal esthetic, or to the latest absurd fashion.

HOME OFFICES is a practical guide for all of those who are thinking about taking this step. This book offers advice and practical examples to help people who work from home – part time or full-time – organize a comfortable, functional, pleasant and practical work space.

HOME OFFICES is divided into six chapters. The first chapter analyzes who chooses to work from home and why. The following four chapters offer guidelines and tips to take the first basic steps in organizing your work from home (choice and planning of space, illumination, storage of material and decoration). The last chapter offers a series of practical examples so the reader may learn from the experience of others who have been through the process of organizing their own office at home.

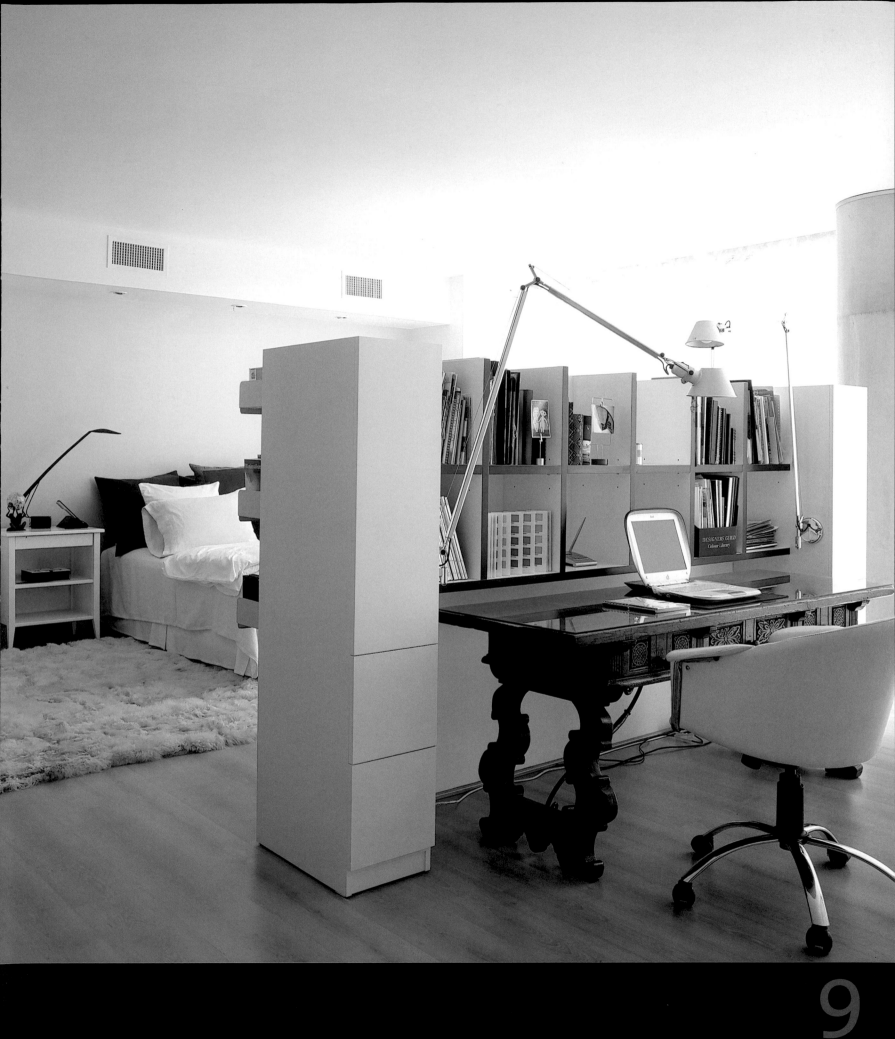

Working from home

Who works from home?

Until only a few years ago, working from home was almost unimaginable. It was considered a rarity often associated with writers and other individuals, easily classified into the 'social eccentrics' category. The center of work was the office, a rigidly centralized and hierarchical space, which was organized, designed and executed with the aim of concentrating the flow of information in one place. The impersonal work spaces as seen in Billy Wilder's film *The Apartment*, have been consolidated in the collective mind as the symbol of a way to work in an ordinary and robotic way, which is unacceptable for many in the 21st century. In a block of flats it is fairly easy to find at least two or three people who spend all or part of their working day at home. Although the obvious candidates to such a privilege are liberal professionals (journalists, designers, architects, lawyers, editors, translators...), the list has been extended to include almost all professional sectors.

There are numerous reasons for this change in the pattern of work, ranging from the technological revolution and the consolidation of the Internet, to the triumph of the Welfare State, which has given citizens increasingly more free time, and even the globalization phenomenon (increased competition between companies from different parts of the world has made it more difficult for these companies to offer jobs for life, as was common around the middle of the last century).

In short, labor mobility and the changes in the leisure pattern have had their effect on the explosion of the phenomenon of working from home. An equally important reason is that more and more people faced with the precarious state of the labor market are responding by turning to self-employment. Moreover, the rise of the price of housing in large city centers has left many with no other option than to move away from big cities. Internet and the great advance in telecommunications have made it possible for these people to remain in the labor market. Nowadays it is common to know of professionals that go to the city but once a week. The center of work, which we have known as the central office until now is, in turn, becoming more of a point of information collection.

An estimated 30% of Europeans and a similar percentage of North American citizens will be working from home before the end of this decade. As this is a relatively new phenomenon, it is hard to find books which explain how to organize this work space. Some architects, not the majority, but a significant number of them, have started to plan their projects taking into account these changes in social habits. The work area can be organized in any room of the house, but in general, and depending on the owner's professional activity, some special light and space conditions are required and a special architectural design is recommended. Obviously, the majority of people cannot afford such a personal design, but keeping in mind some basic guidelines will help avoid this area being an uncomfortable and chaotic space that everyone wants to hide from visitors. Rather, it will help turn this into a place with its own personality and, even, its own particular charm.

In fact, working from home is the final phase, thus far, in a process which began at the end of the 19th century (with the industrial revolution) and the beginning of the 20th century. Back then, the work center *par excellence* was the factory, a place saturated with noise and smoke, chaotic, impersonal, piecework and dehumanizing. It is hard to imagine anything more disheartening than having to go to a factory every morning, including weekends, to do repetitive and mechanical work. Only the high bourgeoisie (bankers, lawyers, doctors...) – the first to work from home, in the modern sense of the term – escaped this destiny.

Little by little, social and technological changes helped ease the heavy burden of industrial work. During the 1960s and 1970s, the idea that a light and friendly workspace helps improve productivity and the worker's state of mind, had already been established. The factory made way for the office, a change for the better, an illuminated, large and colorful space. New theories abound about the use of space, about colors that encourage work and those that discourage, about how to make the rigid hierarchical structures that separate workers from directives less obvious, etc. In short, there is plenty of information about how to make the work space a more pleasant environment.

During the 1980s and 90s, the design of work spaces becomes a doctorate subject at university. The borderline between home and office is blurred and large corporations begin to include gymnasiums, pools, shops and even daycare centers in their work centers.

The so-called aim is that the worker feels less and less removed from the refuge of their home and that the office becomes a kind of extension of this, rather than an aggressive and boring place where the worker is forced to spend a large part of the day. Technological advances make it easier to take part of the work home, as well as doing it all from there.

During the first years of the 21st century, we have taken the next step in this unstoppable revolution of the labor market. Why design offices that are increasingly similar to a home when technological advances make it possible to work from home. The only remaining obstacle, which was fully vanquished a while ago, was the psychological barrier: directives not seeing the worker at their desk through the window of their office. Now it is not so much the physical presence of the worker which is valued as the actual result of their work, which, in most cases, can be discussed and sent by e-mail. Moreover, working from home is supported as much by professional wage workers of large and medium-sized companies who allow them to carry out all or part of their working day at home, as by liberal professionals working as freelancers or without a boss. The image of large masses of people going to their center of work every morning at the same time is already an anachronism true to Fritz Lang's *Metropolis*. In a few years' time, the only ones left in the work centers will be those in charge of coordinating, receiving and distributing the work carried out by those working from home.

Nevertheless, not all jobs can be carried out in a domestic office. The first thing we have to ask ourselves is what we need to be able to do our job. Do we need direct contact with other workers or can we communicate with them via telephone or e-mail? Can we store all the material we need for our professional activity at home or do we need large warehouses or a direct contact with suppliers? Is the furniture and technological equipment we use on a daily basis within our reach or does it surpass our financial abilities? Can we hold the large quantity of peripherals and computer materials needed in the majority of modern jobs? Does working from home involve any unbearable added costs – electricity, telephone, Internet, stationery? As for working with clients or suppliers, do we live close enough to them to be able to attend unexpected meetings easily? Do we have alternative solutions if the computer equipment fails or in case of a domestic hitch? Will we be capable of working completely alone, without a colleague (the extremely sociable can always share their work space with a friend or hire other workers to help them)? And, last but not least, do we have enough discipline to become our own boss without leaving work until the last day? Needless to say the work of a freelancer is not carried out in the same rhythm as that of those who work for others.

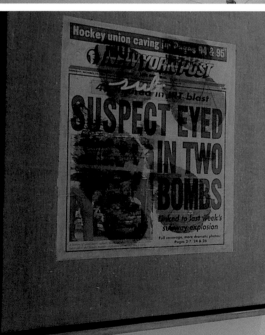

<

The latter receives a salary at the end of every month, while the freelancer risks spending large periods of time without taking in almost anything, which can be de-motivating even for the hardiest among us. Obviously, those wishing to set up their own company have to think about other factors, such as viability, expectations, market research, legal requisites and company plans, which do not correspond to the objectives of this book.

In general (regardless of the purely practical aspects or those related to interior design, which we will address in depth in the following four chapters), any person planning to work from home must take into account both the positive and negative aspects and consequences of their decision.

We must not forget that for every positive aspect, there is always a negative counterpart. For example, against the undeniable virtue of working far away from our bosses we are faced with working alone, without our usual work colleagues. Thus, perhaps we ought to analyze whether we have not underestimated the advantages of the daily brainstorming that occurs unconsciously when we interact with our work colleagues. On the other hand, though there is an advantage to working without the stress associated with big offices, there is also an inevitable tendency for freelancers or liberal professionals to work unusual hours or work into their free time when they organize their work schedule. Although there are fiscal advantages to working from home, there is also the disadvantage of having to spend more on supplies and office materials, not to mention transport costs, especially if our activity will take place in a house located on the outskirts of the city, or the loss of contacts and influence that working from home can entail. It is also more logical for a directive to promote one of his office workers rather than someone who works from home, regardless of how efficient, punctual and professional they may be.

Sharing the work space can be a solution to some of these problems, although it would be preferable to choose someone who works in the same professional sector (as long as this person is not a competitor, of course) over someone whose needs are completely different from ours.

Basically, experience has shown us that the main problem of working from home is not the organization of the work space, but other purely emotional questions, such as self-discipline, the ability to concentrate, perseverance...

A hierarchical environment, as found in an office, helps to maintain a rhythm and a continued motivation in time, while an office at home can quickly lead to de-motivation or can become too comfortable, not forgetting the usual distractions of the home, such as children, friends, television... The temptation to stop work for a while to take a short break, which turns into a longer than recommended break, is something that presents itself on a daily basis. If there is a lack of discipline, one can end up working into the small hours, which, obviously, is akin to getting out of the frying pan and into the fire.

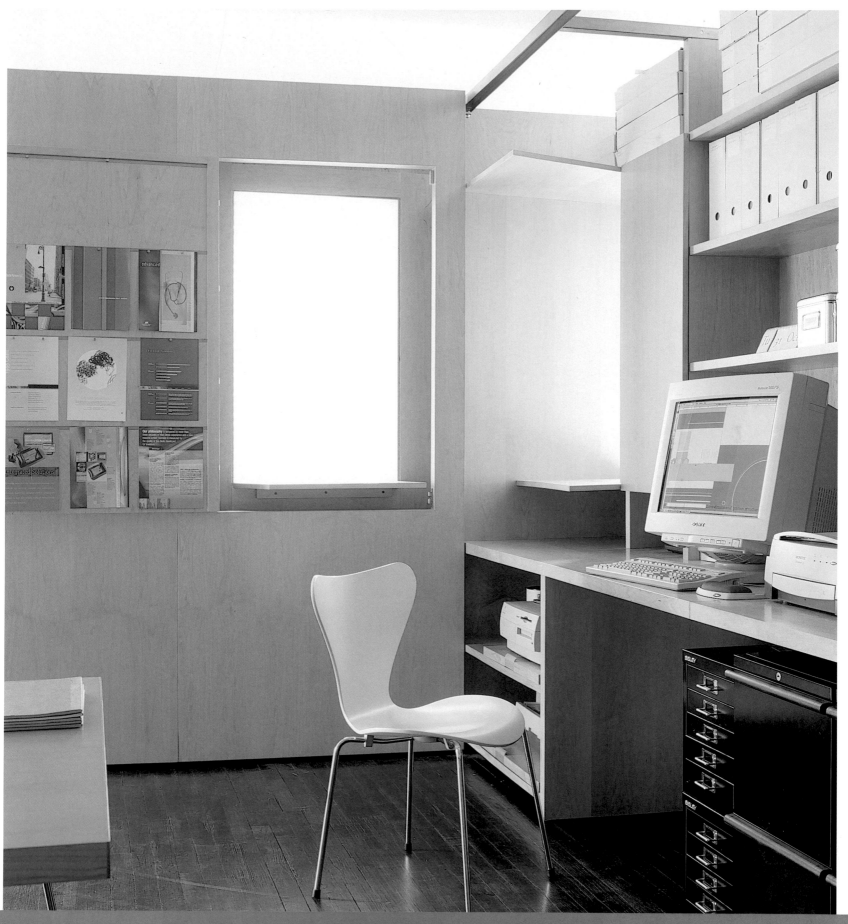

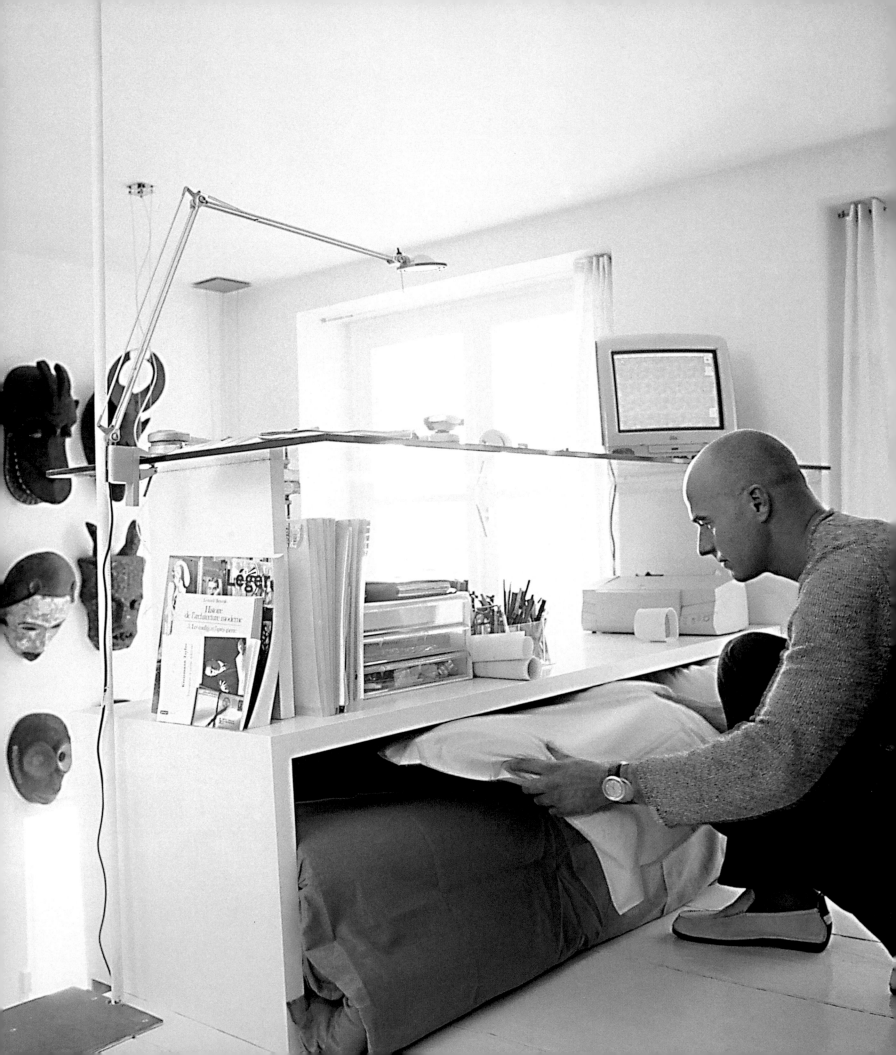

Organizing the space

Good ideas, bad ideas

After weighing up the pros and cons, we have decided to organize our own work space at home. Obviously, the first step is to find the appropriate place. One of the most common mistakes at this point of the process is wanting to hide the work space in some isolated corner of the house, out of the way and relatively hidden from view. Maybe we consider our work to be a heavy burden and unconsciously try to confine it to a small corner of the house in order to forget about it when we are not immersed in it. In this case, perhaps the best solution is to change jobs first, rather than try to hide the work space as much as possible. Or, perhaps we want to respect and preserve the personality of the rest of the house and not introduce a discordant element. In this case, it is useful to remember one basic rule of interior decoration: it is not recommendable to try and hide large elements as the result is often much more visually disastrous than leaving them on view and trying to integrate them. In any case, who said that a work space cannot have its own personality and even become one of the house's major appealing features?

Once again, if we consider our work is an activity far removed from our "real" life, perhaps we should start thinking about making changes in our life rather than try and work miracles with interior design. It is one thing wanting to dedicate an entire room of the house to the work space in order to be able to close the door at the end of the work day and forget about it, but quite another to try and hide it. The first option is quality of life; the second, a determined escape.

To choose the appropriate place to work, we must first be very clear on what our professional needs are. Do we need natural light? Do we need a large table or can we manage with a simple desk? Do we have a large amount of material to file away or do we rely on a digital source which takes up a ridiculous amount of space? Do we need a socket nearby for the telephone? Do we spend 100% of our time at home, or only part of it? We must keep in mind that we are designing our own space based on our own needs, and not those of others, thus it need not resemble, nor do we want this, the cubicles of the companies where we have worked in the past. There are no written rules that tell us desks must have a draw beneath it or that the telephone must be on the right-hand side of the keyboard. These seem to be logical solutions (and they are, for the most part), but we do not have to follow them strictly if we are more comfortable with other possibilities.

The basic rules we must apply to our work space are much more generic: good illumination, be it natural or artificial; a large table or, at least large enough for our needs; a comfortable chair; room for filing and storing work material of different sizes; and, lest we forget, a pleasant esthetic which motivates us to work. The specific details, on the other hand, are left to the discretion of the user.

It is important not to underestimate our assessments. The objects that surround us tend to take up all the available space, however big this may be, thus it is better to work out that we will need at least 50% more of the space that we initially predicted. It is also important to know that a journalist, who will no doubt have to store a large amount of papers, books and magazines (objects of medium size and a lot of weight) will not have the same needs as a computer technician, who will work almost exclusively with the computer and few more objects and peripherals. It is also advisable to spend a little extra time strategically planning the work space. If we use the printer on a daily basis, it is best to have it nearby, perhaps on the work table itself or on an auxiliary table. If we use it once a month, it won't matter if we place it in a more inconvenient place (on a table further away, a large bookcase or even on the floor).

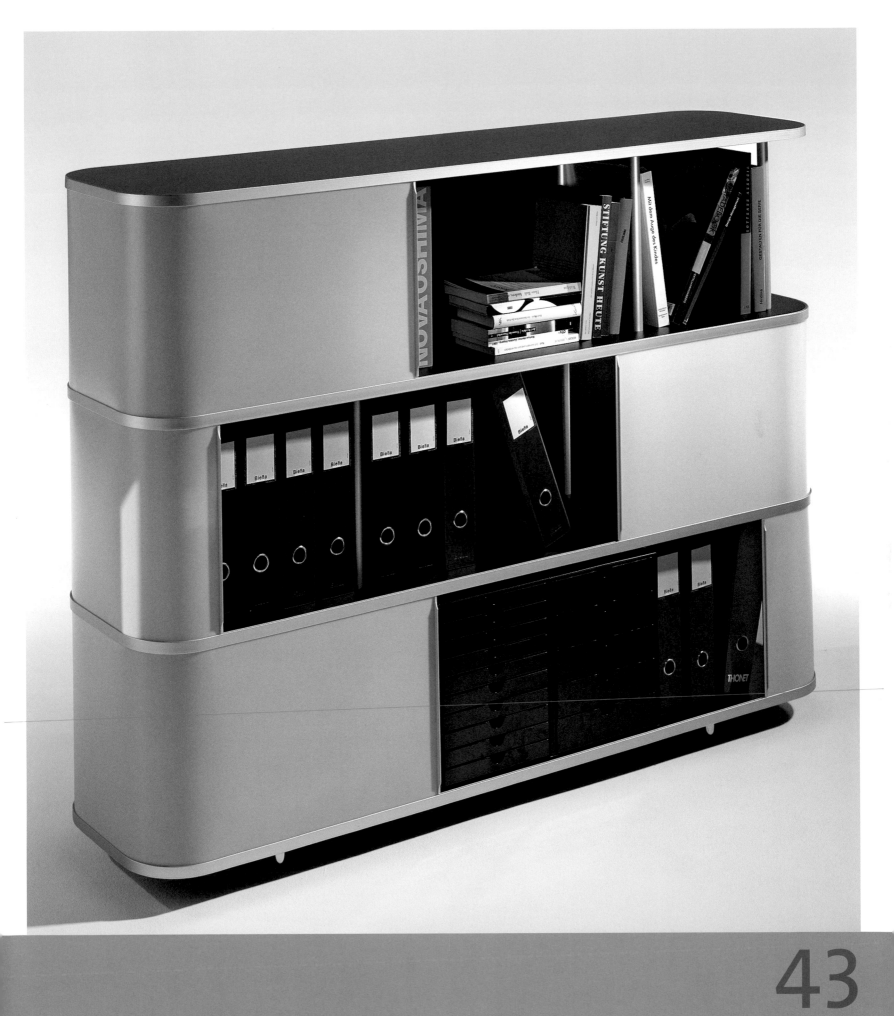

43

For those who live in small apartments or who very seldom work at home and, though this may seem contradictory, prefer a work space that doesn't take up any room, there are practical solutions, not particularly cheap ones, though not excessively expensive either, such as, for example panels hidden in the wall, similar to folding beds, or even partial solutions such as separating screens or placing a small plank and a chest of drawers inside a little used built-in cupboard.

Another thing to consider is whether the work area is for our sole use or to be shared with others (our partner, for example), or whether we plan to hire someone to work for us in this same space. Obviously, in both cases, the space will need to be doubled, or even tripled, as the room required for one person is not the same when it needs to be shared. Will we receive regular visits from clients or suppliers? If so, we may need to sacrifice a certain comfort, because the chaos in which we are perfectly happy, may convey a bad image of us as professionals. Will we hold meetings with other colleagues? In this case we will need a large space to be able to do so comfortably. Will we always work with the computer or will we need other kinds of furniture? An office is not only made up of a desk and some shelves, perhaps we will need a sofa, more chairs, a meeting table, lamps, an extra table, waste bins, drawers, etc.

Though lighting in the work space will be addressed in another chapter of the book, it is important to bear in mind that it is always better to work with natural light than with artificial light. For those lucky enough to have a well-lit house, it should be no a problem to find an appropriate work space. However, if light is limited, we may prefer to use the house's bright rooms for the dining or living room rather than the office. Nevertheless, wherever possible, it is always better to work in spaces with natural light.

Finally, we need to decide whether we want the decoration of our work space to integrate with the rest of the house, or whether we prefer it to give it its own personality. Obviously, a work space has its own rules. Here, contrary to other rooms in the house, function is more important than esthetics. However, this is usually not even considered a dilemma by good interior designers, for whom function and esthetics are not contradictory or opposite terms, but complementary.

Try it out for yourself. If you move the computer from your work space, does it look like this is an extra room of the house or does it clearly reveal its function. Both options are completely valid, you just have to decide whether you choose to integrate your work space or separate it. In any case, the personalization of the space completely depends on each user's type of activity. For example, a lawyer may be able to integrate his work space into the rest of the house more easily than a photographer, who needs to work with small buckets of liquid and whose work is essentially more manual, or an architect who needs large work tables.

Also, it wouldn't be bad to take into consideration those details that attract our attention when we leaf through decoration magazines or books. We have all seen the huge lawyers' offices in Hollywood films. Why do they attract our attention? Because of their large windows, their cozy fitted carpets, their huge and spacious desks, the careful lighting, dark wooden furniture, the huge plants and paintings that give the place a touch of personality and distinction... It may just be a set, but let us be practical, is it not possible to design our own work space with these details in mind? In the same films, we have seen those huge rooms, almost like industrial warehouses, full of cloned cubicles with masses of impersonal clerks. What is it that disgusts us about these cubicles? Perhaps it is the

artificial light, the claustrophobic feeling they provoke, the absence of color and warmth, the size and dehumanization, the noise from nearby cubicles, the outrageous furniture...

We must remember that there are no written rules for the small details of our work area, but one must also take into think about the things that tend to work with some logic, at least in interior design. An ugly desk is not only ugly in esthetic terms. Unconsciously, its ugliness probably suggests it will be an uncomfortable table or difficult to integrate or to combine with other furniture. A shelf that is too deep may create a powerful esthetic, but if we want the spines of all our books to be on view, we may find ourselves with a huge empty space behind these books, which could be used to store other elements. Perhaps we are not convinced by having a chest of drawers next to our legs (who has not knocked their knee at some point), but, in the end, if this is the place it has been for decades, is it not because it is the most logical and appropriate place for it? There is another, completely different, danger: overrating our needs. Maybe we don't really need that much space, such a big table, kilometers of shelves... Perhaps all we need is a simple computer table and some shelves for our limited office material and document resources. In this case, the best thing would be to buy a desk especially designed to meet our needs.

There are companies that produce tables and extra modules that are completely compatible. If you want to do away with the drawers and, instead, insert a small extendable platform for the printer, you can.

Don't rule out any space completely without having weighed up its pros and cons. That hard-to-furnish corner, which has been a nuisance more than anything else until now, could be the perfect work space. Or that room with the inclined ceiling where you can hardly stand up straight. Or that dead corner in the kitchen. Or the basement or the garage. Or that space under the stairs where you tend to store boxes full of annoying junk. Or the attic. A dead wall may turn out to be ideal for long shelves to store hundreds of books. Any nook and cranny can function perfectly as a work space, although, naturally, it will always be more difficult to transform one of those uncomfortable spaces on a limited budget.

A custom-built shelf will always be more expensive than a mass-produced one with standard measurements, not to mention the structural adjustments. If our space is not purely a center of work, but also serves as an office in which to receive visitors or hold meetings, perhaps it would be a good idea to get an estimate to convert what was a simple apartment into a home with a double use, rather than messing about trying to find an intermediate solution, which will probably end up being not only temporary but also unsatisfactory.

A good piece of advice to keep in mind: if you are prepared to undertake important structural reforms, think about whether the final result will add value to your home or will take away from it. It may be that a provisionally satisfactory result may not be so in a few years' time, when you move to another home and are forced to sell your flat. Perhaps potential buyers won't see the need for a room fitted out as a work space. Or, perhaps they do need this, in which case the value of your home will increase beyond what you have spent in reforming it.

Though we cannot know how the property market of your city will evolve in the next ten years, we can be almost 100% certain that the number of people working from home will progressively increase during this period. Therefore, the answer to your doubts is, go ahead!

Don't underestimate the value of good furniture, especially a quality desk and chair. An uncomfortable desk and chair can make any pleasant job horrible. Obviously, the best desks and chairs are not cheap, but the result will more than compensate what you pay for them. Leave designer chairs for the living room. The appropriate chair for you is more likely to resemble one out of Star Trek's *Enterprise* space ship, rather than what you tend to consider a 'nice chair'. Adjustable arms, back and height should be almost compulsory. A good chair is one that forces you to keep your back in an S-like position, the most natural position of the vertebral column. Despite a good chair, you will still need to get up once in a while to rest your back. Also, decide whether you want a chair with wheels, which will allow you to move from one side of the room to the other easily, or whether you prefer no wheels, which will give you more stability. The same can be said for the desk, which should neither be too high nor too low. Place the desk at the distance of your wrists with your arms stretched out and your back resting against the chair's back. When you are tapping on the computer's keyboard, your arms should be at an angle of 90 degrees. Your desktop should be more or less at the height of your elbow when you are sitting down. Basically, your desk should be large and solid.

Another element that deserves special attention if you want a pleasant and organized space is your storage system (cupboards, drawers, shelves and filing cabinets...). Although this will be dealt with in more detail in another chapter, it is good to keep this in mind when you are planning the layout of your work space. So, you must ask yourself what kind of material you want to or must store and what kind of furniture you need for this. If you are a translator perhaps you need a bookshelf exclusively for dictionaries with some filing cabinets and shelves to keep CDs with back-ups, or the paperwork you generate, etc. If you are a painter, though, you will probably need filing cabinets for large pieces of paper and cupboards for pots of pigment, brushes, cloth and other utensils. Depending on your needs, you will require one type of furniture or another. Bookcases are very practical and allow you to store elements of different sizes, including books, boxes, files, videos, etc. As well as bookcases, there are cupboards or low pieces of furniture with doors. These are perfect to keep boxes or other objects we do not wish to have on view, as they clash with the decoration of the space or because they are too big to place in bookcases with standard measurements. Another possibility is to close bookcases with glass doors, so we can easily find the things we are looking for and, at the same time, these give the space a kind of energy preventing our office from turning into a continued succession of plain doors which visually cram the room. Also consider that doors avoid the accumulation of dust and dirt and that (if opaque) they protect the more fragile materials from the light. Furniture with doors can provide a variety of possibilities within a work space. If the furniture is low, it can be placed beneath the window, making the most of a space that would otherwise not be used, or they can be hung on the wall, thus gaining floor space. The final choice will depend on your needs and preferences. Another element often used in the office area is shelves. Their versatility have made them a very popular element in work spaces. To decide where to put them, you must take into account what you will use them for, which objects you will place on them and whether you want them within your reach or, if not, whether you will put decorative or little used elements on them. As mentioned before, all of this will determine their location. You can place them above the desk, on the wall, or even above doors and windows. If you are sure what they will be used for, you can also decide the appropriate width.

A chest of drawers is very useful and almost essential. Be it underneath your desk or next to it, this is where you will be able to store office materials, paper, files, etc. There is a great variety and you can find them with drawers of different heights, with rails for hanging files, etc. Some have wheels, which is a practical solution that lets us move them and thus change the distribution of the study according to our needs.

If the space is large enough, you will be able to store a large number of books, documents, files, etc. If you have limited room, however, you will have to ask yourself if you really need everything that you want to store. In the end, this restriction can be beneficial as it will make you discriminate between what is important and what isn't and will make you be stricter about your organization. In this sense , a certain order, at least self-order, will make your work easier, the day-to-day less tedious and will result in a more pleasant and productive surrounding. For example, if the bills are classified in files, you will not have any problem finding them when you need them. Although it seems obvious, it is worth insisting and creating good habits for storing your materials. Always keep your correspondence in the same tray or the office material in the same drawer, for example, and thus enjoy your time and space better.

The almost infinite variety of materials, forms and colors, of both furniture and storage utensils, will allow you to create a personalized work space. Depending on the system you use, you will obtain different effects and an esthetic better adapted to your own personality.

65

Avoid narrow desktops, however vanguard they may seem, as well as those made of flexible materials. Work out yourself how much space your material will take up (computer, keyboard, mouse, loudspeakers, telephone, books...) and multiply this by three or four to work out how much space you will need. Your legs should fit underneath the table without the problem of knocking your knees every time you get close to the desk with your chair. If you are planning on using a large amount of peripherals on a desk which rests against the wall, you may need a desktop with small holes through which to pass the cables. Do not discard tables in irregular shapes – L-shaped or curved – as they may be more appropriate than a traditional rectangular table.

It is always a good idea to draw a small sketch of the work space and the elements that will take up this area, as it will help you quickly visualize the different ways of organizing. If you still have the plans of the house, it will be easier to draw the furniture on top of these and check if the measurements fit. Don't forget to take into account the power points and telephone sockets. If you place a desk against a wall without power points you will have to leave some cables hanging and risk tripping up, or use inconvenient and excessive extension leads. If you have found the ideal corner or room for your work space, but it lacks power points, you will have to make the installation reach this point. Therefore, you may need to add the electrician's estimate to your initial provision of expenses.

When planning the organization of the elements of your work space, you must keep in mind some basic rules. Do not dismiss any composition of furniture, however eccentric it may seem. Sometimes we are too blinded by what we already know that we reject creative and useful solutions because of their apparent heterodoxy. Place the main elements (chair and table) and the largest ones (sofa, shelves, drawers) before the smaller items. Check how far the natural light reaches, which corners are darkest and which are better illuminated, saving the first for filing and material storage and the second for reading areas and work. Place what you use more frequently as close as possible to the desk. Make sure the computer screen is not facing the sun, as the reflection will make it difficult for you to read the screen properly, it is much better if you are facing the window. Do not limit yourself to placing furniture against the room's walls, you are organizing a work space not making room for a dance floor. If you are going to work with a colleague, you should think about whether you want to sit next to them, face them or have your back to them. Finally, put all the elements in their place and check their function. After a couple of months working in this space on a daily basis you will realize what you got right and what you got wrong: perhaps you don't use the fax that takes up so much room all that much or perhaps it would be better to have the pot of pens and pencils closer at hand, even though you mainly work with the computer. In fact, it is almost impossible to get the organization of

the work elements right the first time round. And if you do, maybe that's because this is not the first work space you have organize, in which case, experience is a fine thing.

Do not forget to keep a space for yourself in your home office, and for all those who will, at some point or another, have to share this with you. There is nothing more uncomfortable and, which gives a feeling of disorganization, as having to hold a formal work meeting and having to bring chairs in from other rooms of the house or having to move boxes and drawers out of the way at the last minute, so that visitors can come through. We cannot all be lucky enough to have a huge sunny room as a work area, but we can all organize its elements in the most comfortable, logical and functional way possible. Last but not least, think about your obsessions. You can't stand the slightest bit of noise while you work? Or, on the contrary, you need to listen to music while you work? In this case, save room for your music equipment and the CDs you will listen to most frequently. Are you obsessed with order or, do you need a certain amount of chaos around you from which to extract new ideas? Don't underestimate your own obsessions, as long as these are inoffensive. Most of time these are small unconscious aides which your mind and body request in order to improve their performance at work.

Basic principles

If it is good for a plant, it should be good for you. This is the basic principle to follow when trying to find the best lighting for our work space (ferns and other similar plants are the exception to the rule). They need much less light than you). Of course, the ideal room would be one with enough natural light reaching every corner and allowing you to read without any difficulties and without the need for extra light sources. If we are not lucky enough to have a space with these characteristics, perhaps we should spend more time thinking about how best to illuminate the work area. An excess of light is not recommendable either, especially if we spend most of our time in front of the computer screen. The basic rule in this case would be to place the back of the computer screen facing the source of natural light. If this is not possible, due to the distinct arrangement of our work space, we can always purchase one of those filters or visors, which can be found in any more or less well stocked computer store. In any case, natural light alone is not enough. One must always count on additional light sources for the days when the sun is not shining or, simply, for working at night.

A natural source of light offers two types of benefits, practical and emotional ones. Practical benefits can be obtained by other means, such as lamps or any other artificial spotlight. Emotional benefits are a little harder to get through any other system imaginable. A number of studies have proved that sunlight improves our state of mind and helps us adopt a positive attitude towards work and those surrounding us. One could say that humans have a similar process to that of the photosynthesis of plants, although in this case the benefits we get from contact with sunlight are more... intangible. Never underestimate the virtues of a good large window. If you think you are receiving more light than you wish, perhaps you should opt for a curtain or some blinds or something similar which will allow you to regulate the intensity of the incoming light. With an excess or lack of light you will frown constantly, which could eventually lead to unbearable headaches. As everybody has a relatively different sensibility to light, depending on the color of your eyes for example, you should take into account your specific needs. Do not let yourself be influenced by what others think is more appropriate for you, as you are the only one who knows how much light you need to work.

Artificial light sources imitate, or pretend to imitate, natural light. Always try to work with direct or indirect lights aimed at very

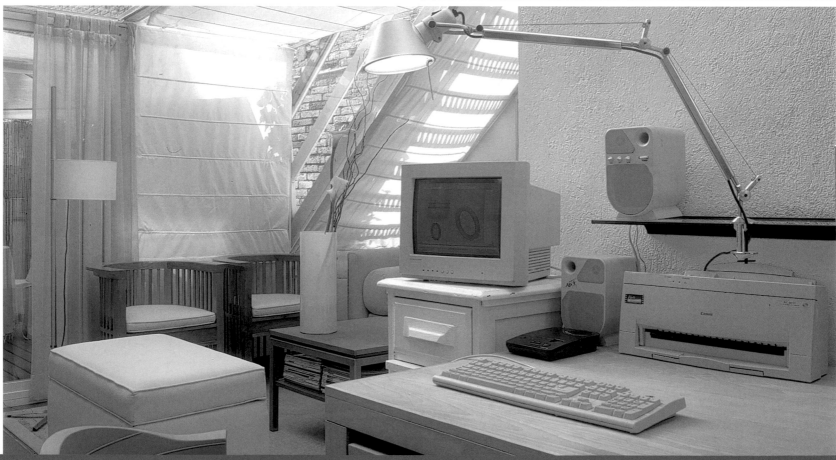

specific areas of your work space, and never direct the light towards your eyes. If you do not have a natural source of light and you have to resort to artificial lamps and spotlights, try to combine "practical" lights, which only illuminate the work area, with "atmospheric" lights, which illuminate only a little but help give the environment a touch of warmth, making it esthetically more pleasing. There are hundreds of lamps and spotlights that easily adapt to almost any chosen furniture arrangement. Some have extendable feet and arms, others allow you to adjust the intensity of the light, some can be screwed into the wall, table or any other flat surface... You would be hard pressed not to find the kind of lamp or spot you are looking for in any specialized shop. As a final resort, and budget-permitting, you could always have a specific lighting system installed in your work space, although it would be hard to imagine that this peculiar configuration of lights you have chosen cannot be found in a more conventional and, more importantly, cheaper way.

Whenever possible, try to place your work space in rooms or corners of the house that are north-facing (if you live in the planet's northern hemisphere). Light from the north is less aggressive and clearer than light from the south, although the latter also provides more warmth. East-facing rooms will receive light in the morning and at noon, but not in the afternoon, while in west-facing rooms the opposite will happen, naturally. Our advice is that you paint the walls in light colors – preferably white – to make the most of the light, especially if you live in countries with little sunlight. White and light colors reflect and multiply light, which bounces off against these colors, while dark colors kill the light, and also make a room seem smaller than it actually is. The same happens with textured paints (such as stucco, for example) or patterned wallpaper.

We have already told you to opt for natural light wherever possible and complementing this with artificial spotlights. Keep in mind that not all artificial lights are the same and that not all of them produce the same kind of light. We are not talking about the strength of the spotlight, but about the quality and the type of light it emits. As a general rule, avoid fluorescent lights, unless you want your work space to resemble a pretty depressing-looking surgery room. If these have traditionally been used by directors of horror movies to induce a frightened or claustrophobic state of mind in the viewer, there is a reason for this. However, there are more and more models of fluorescent lights which prove that this cliché is not totally true, or that at least these lights are changing. Traditional light bulbs emit a yellowish kind of light, which is not too aggressive. If you prefer a more powerful light, opt for halogen lights, which are more expensive, but also more durable. There are also low energy bulbs, which are much more durable than the ones mentioned before, though they considerably more expensive.

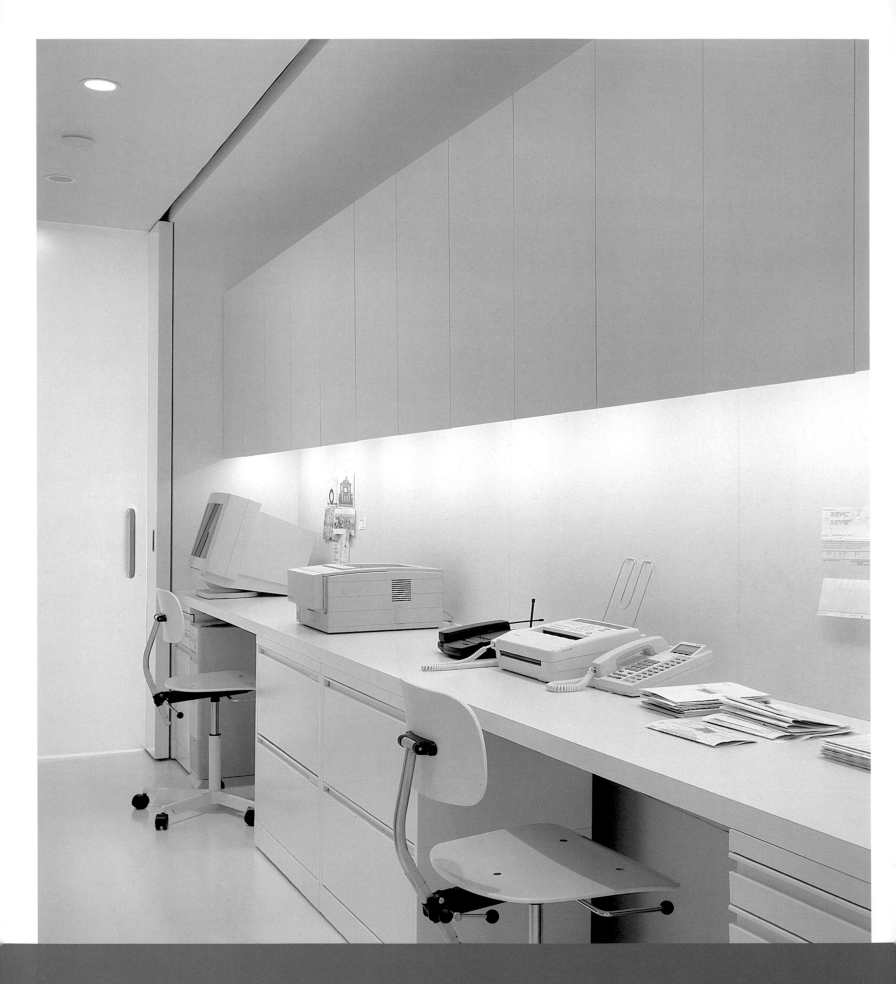

It is important to think about the direction of the lights that we install in our work space. Facing the ceiling, from bottom to top, the light will be blurred and will seem less aggressive, which may be the best solution for powerful lights with a wide range (in other words, those with a spotlight that resemble a cone). The whole workspace will be equally illuminated by lights placed in the ceiling or high up and facing downwards. These should be the main lights and which provide the minimum amount of illumination needed to work comfortable. The directionality of lights – of medium power and with a focus similar to a tube – must be used to illuminate an area of particular point of our work space, for example that corner of the table which we use to examine the negatives of our photos. Table lamps are an example of these as they illuminate a small space, although they do not focus a particular point. Finally, we can install one or more purely decorative lamps, which will illuminate almost nothing, but which will give the work space a pleasant feeling.

Don't forget that a light that is too strong and badly directed can do more harm than good, as it can create areas that are too bright and others that are completely dark. Perhaps these areas are not really that dark (they could be illuminated by another lamp) but

the contrast between one normal light and another exaggerated one can make your eyes perceive the less lit area as something similar to a well.

As it takes time for our eyes to adjust to different degrees of brightness, making them change focus constantly or making them adjust from one very illuminated area to another less illuminated one quickly and often, will soon create sight problems and headaches. Therefore we recommend stronger lamps that come with adjusters, to modify the strength. Shades can also help tone down lights that are too strong. However, when using very strong lamps, one must be careful not to use easily flammable shades, like paper ones, for example. Do not forget to illuminate all corners of your work space. One of the most common mistakes is to only worry about the lights that illuminate the desk, forgetting about shelves where the books, files or necessary office supplies are stored. Remember that a large part of your time will be spent looking for papers or books on these shelves, so they should be well-lit. Finally, try to use one or more lamps with a flexible foot so that they can be directed to different areas of the work space, as and when required. Spotlights with clips are good options, as they can be placed almost anywhere.

In short, think of your work space as a lively, flexible, adaptable and constantly changing place, rather than as a mausoleum. It is always better that the different pieces of furniture adapt to you rather than you feeling forced to adapt to them.

A place for everything

Get organized or die! This may seem
exaggerated, but it cannot be stressed
enough. Thus, when planning our work space,
we must dedicate all the time necessary to
think about how we are going to organize
the work itself, how we plan to organize and
arrange the supplies and documents needed
for our activity, what we will use most
frequently, what we will use sporadically
and, of course, how much room we have.
If our office is going to be in a separate room,
we must decide whether all that which is
related to our work activity will be confined
to this room. If, on the other hand, the office
will be integrated in one of the rooms of the
home, such as the bedroom or living room, we
must try and integrate the boxes and files into
the decoration of the home or at least make
sure they can be hidden inside a cupboard or
something similar kind of piece of furniture.

But, let's take it step by step. The first thing, as mentioned before, is to know what it is we want to store. If the room is large, it may not be necessary to consider this, but what happens if the study is small or if it has to be shared with several people? Do we really need everything that we want to store? When organizing the studio it could be the perfect occasion to do away with obsolete papers, old diaries and junk that we end up accumulating without knowing how or why. Once we have thought about the elements we must save, file and classify, it will be much easier to choose the appropriate pieces of furniture and decide on the best distribution for the study. Good planning, where every object and document has its place, has other advantages too. For example, at the end of the working day, it will be much quicker and simpler to put everything in its place to find a tidy and clean space the following day, which will make it easier for us to return to our tasks, not to mention the embarrassment an unexpected visit from a client or supplier could cause if our space is not in a perfect, magazine-style, state.

When choosing storage material, the esthetic can be an important aim, though we must never forget that function is the main aim. You must be able to move around easily and be comfortable. A fabulous little designer cupboard in which the folders of the size you require do not fit will not be useful at all. In the same way, if you lose out on the spaciousness of the

hallway by placing some very convenient chest of drawers there, you may need to re-think its location in a less conflictive space.

Luckily there are plenty of places to find the appropriate kinds of storage furniture with a huge variety of designs, materials and prices available. From pieces of furniture intended and designed especially for offices, but which can be adapted to our home, to furniture originally intended for the home, such as desks and compact pieces of furniture which can easily work as office furniture.

With a little bit of patience, you are sure to find those pieces that adjust to your needs and budget. You could even opt for a bit of DIY and make your own pieces of furniture using some wood and metal pieces. Anything is allowed, as long as the result reflects exactly what it is you need.

The bookcase is a versatile and almost omnipresent element, which can hold books, files, folders, etc. and is often used in offices. Unlike shelves, which tend to be placed individually, bookcases make up larger units that help define the style of a room. The esthetic of these pieces of furniture can characterize the decoration of a work space. A lawyers or doctors' office, perhaps more classical with its elegant and valuable wooden bookcases, is not the same as the office of graphic designers, where we find a more

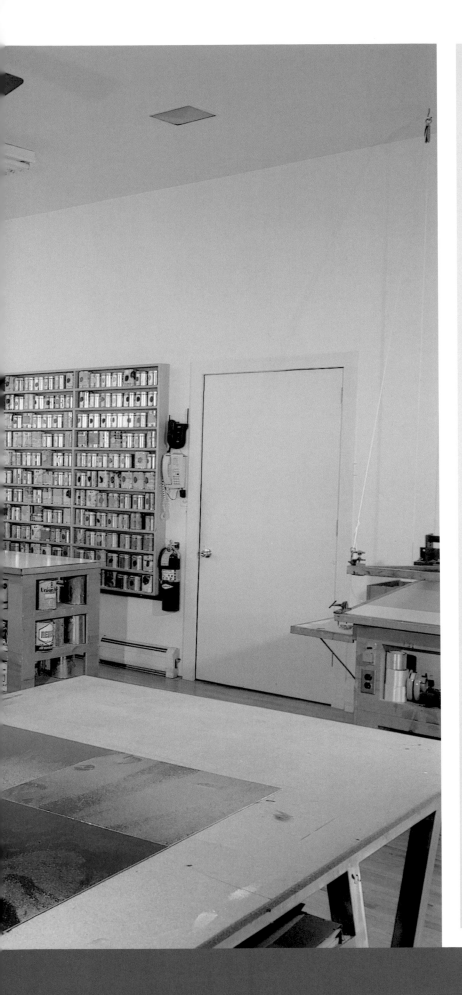

imaginative and care-free style and use of materials. Regardless of the preference, though, one must think about the height of this piece of furniture, for example. We must consider whether we want it to reach the ceiling in order to make the most of the available space, or whether we prefer it to be lower. We must also think about how many shelves we want, what we are going to put in the bookcase (books, CD, DVD, magazines...), whether it will have doors or not, etc. If it has doors, it is worth remembering that glass doors protect the inside from dust and also allows us to easily find what we are looking for, while opaque doors help protect the contents from the light and also help us hide the content. This last option can create a boring environment, especially if the result is a succession of plain doors that are all the same. A good solution could be to use translucent doors or a combination of opaque and transparent doors.

Shelves are another important piece of furniture in the studio. These are almost indispensable in any office and are available in a wide range of materials, shapes and colors, as well as being adaptable to almost any space. Shelves can be placed almost anywhere: above the desk to keep office supplies, against a wall for books or folders and even in places which are less accessible but can be ideal to store the material that is used less frequently. Thus, shelves can be placed above doors or windows and, yes, even in that corner next to the column that seems to be so useless. To adjust them to the available space in our studio, all that needs to be done is to modify the length and depth of the shelf. Shelves adapt to any kind of material we want to store, from the typical folders to tins of paint, photographic material, boxes of different sizes or CDs, for example. When putting up the shelves, one must think about the kind of supports or the support system we will be using. There are a number of possibilities, including shelves with invisible supports, metal shelf supports, different materials and designs for squares and angles, etc. It is worth remembering that the kind of support must bear some relation to the weight and size of the objects that will be placed on the shelf. So, if the shelf has to bear a heavy load, it is better to use shelves of a certain thickness and as many supports as necessary to ensure its stability, otherwise it can start to bend over time, or, worse still, can break under the weight of its contents. The infinite number of designs for shelves and supports mean these can adapt to any decorative style: elegant glass shelves, robust solid wood shelves or conspicuous colorful plywood shelves.

There are two more elements that seem to be present in work spaces: chests of drawers and filing cabinets. These very handy pieces of furniture can solve a number of storage problems. A chest of drawers can be placed beneath the desk, thus freeing up space, and can be used to store supplies used on a daily basis, so that they are within easy reach, such as note blocks and diaries. You can even choose furniture on wheels, which you can move around as you wish, either because you want to clean underneath, or because you like to change the arrangement of the furniture in the office every once in a while.

The filing cabinet, the other great classic, allows you to organize all the documents and files you generate during your professional activity. The widespread use of this element has generate a great variety of sizes and materials to completely satisfy almost any request. For example, they are available in wood, metal, plastic, with or without wheels, with several levels, with locks, for sheets of paper, for videotapes, for architecture plans, for dossiers, for small filing cards, etc. All varieties have one fundamental thing in common: the material filed inside is quickly and easily accessed.

So far, we have talked about large and medium-sized office furniture, about different types of containers, basically. However, equally important when working, are what we can call small pieces of furniture, that which lives inside the drawers, rests on the shelves, swarms the desk, sits inside the folders etc. We are talking about files, boxes, covers, pencil boxes, trays, etc. If we found a huge variety of models in the previous sections, the variety here is almost infinite. This small filing system can easily be found in stationer's or specialized shops. The model will depend on the style you choose for your work space, and more importantly, it will help you organize your documents. For example, you can use different colored folders to differentiate the type of papers you want to store, such as dispatch notes, bills, estimates, signed contracts, etc. Or perhaps the colors can be used to separate the documents by year. Whatever your choice, appropriately using the shapes and colors available for this kind of material can help you maintain order in your work area, as well as giving you an added tool to mark the esthetic of your study. If you want a dynamic and contemporary space, choose striking colors. If, on the other hand, you want a relaxed space, light and soft colors will work best.

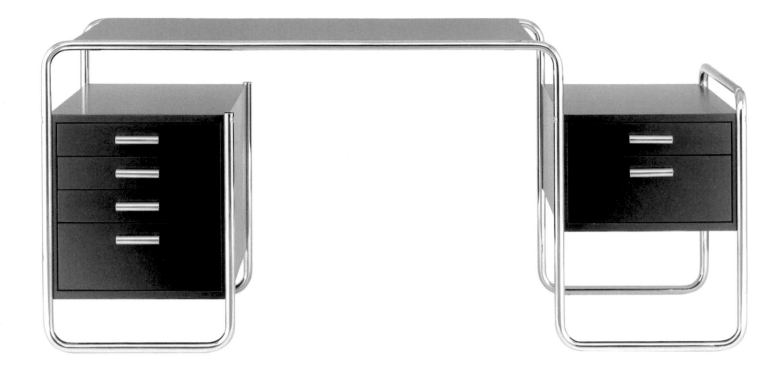

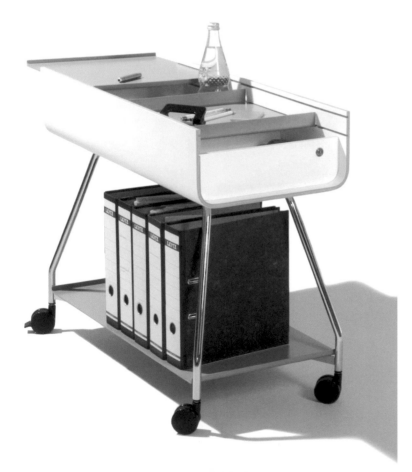

Safety is, in some way, related to office furniture and the order and arrangement of storage components. We often feel that our home is a kind of refuge where nothing bad can happen to us, a place where we are safe from accidents. Statistics, however, prove the opposite. We do not mean to alarm you, but we do not want you to be overconfident, either. There are certain aspects of health and safety at work that affect the external office as much as the home office, and which must be taken into consideration. First of all, there are the risks which stem from bad posture. Correct ergonomics are fundamental if we want to avoid small pains or ending up in the hands of a physiotherapist. Therefore, if you spend lots of time in front of the computer, as well as having a good work chair, perhaps we should consider a foot rest and one of those systems that help you rest your wrists. Nowadays it is almost impossible to find a work space that does not use some kind of electricity. It is obvious why and we are not going to wax lyrical about this source of energy, but it is important, however, that we do not forget its dangers. It is essential that all the cables of the equipment you use (computers, screens, printers and faxes, telephones, extra lamps, etc.) and their corresponding sockets are in good condition. Try to avoid cables crossing the work space, making it easy to trip up. There are a number of options both for the extension and tidying up of cables. Another important aspect is the correct distribution of the furniture. If everything is where it should be you will obtain a fluid problem-free space with a good circulation of people and you will be able to annoying cuts and bruises. Also remember that if you have to store boxes or files in high places, you must use a ladder or other system that will ensure your security. These small falls are more frequent than you can imagine.

And finally, keep in mind that inappropriate air-conditioning and cleaning in the work space, let's say a lack hereof, can affect our ability to work. Clean air, regularly renewed, and avoiding the accumulation of dust can save you from future breathing complications or allergies.

Decoration

**Customizing the work space.
Decorative details**

To fuse or to separate. These are not the
pre-election slogans of two political parties,
rather they are the two options we have
when thinking about the decoration and
customization of our work space, choosing
to isolate or integrate it into the surrounding
space. The first solution will reassert the
independent character of the work area,
while the second choice may seem less risky
but also more in harmony with that which
surrounds it.

At first, the decoration of our work space may not seem so important, in comparison with its planning, distribution, organization and illumination. However, if it is not that important, then why do we insist on decorating our house in such a way that it reflects our tastes? Basically, because an elegant, functional, stimulating and harmonious decoration helps us feel better. So, why should it be any different for our work space? Anyone who has worked in the offices of large companies will know how frustrating it is not being able to change the decoration of their 'territory', except for the tiniest details. The decoration of the offices of any company is generally chosen to suit a standard, average taste, in accordance with a series of behavior and emotional motivation rules, which do not necessarily apply to everyone. These kinds of interior design are completely neutral, they are not particularly pleasant or unpleasant, though completely the opposite. but is the opposite.

Our work space, on the other hand, can be modeled, livened up and decorated however we want it. A sweet-toothed goal, but also a very deceitful one. It is one thing to personalize the space in which we are going to work throughout most of the day, and quite another to fall into the interior design delirium just for the sake of it.

Before we definitely begin to work, we must remember that we are going to customize our office, not create an artistic installation. And though we are the first to encourage any interior designer at heart to try out and test new ideas, we will also remind the more adventurous that if nobody has invented lime soup until now, there is a reason for this. Sobriety does not equal boring, just as classic does is not always mean conservative. A space that is too loud can distract us from what is really important – our work – while a space that is too plain or minimalist can end up subduing even the most creative and high-spirited professionals.

There is nothing stopping you from working in something similar to a cube of plain walls or inside a Dalí painting, though perhaps an intermediate solution between pure functionality and unleashed and irrational creativity may be more satisfying in the long run. Finally, remember, fashions come... and go, and what is 'in' now will most probably seem ridiculous in a few years' time.

Do not try to decorate your space from start to finish on the first day. Let it come to life little by little, and let it decide for itself what suits it. Also think about all those who will be passing through. Are you planning on receiving clients? Will you share the space with other people? Will your partner also be using the space? If so, take into account the tastes of others and the impression you want to give those that will be judging you, in part, by the esthetic of your office. If the esthetic were not really that important, companies would not take care in designing attractive packaging for their products and you would not be obliged to dress appropriately for a job interview, for example. Don't be fooled, image is important and it sells.

Think about what makes you feel comfortable. Surrounding yourself with cushions so that you can take your little breaks among them may be a bad idea in a company where the socially acceptable break consists of have a coffee or smoking a cigarette on a terrace that is windblown first thing in the morning. However, who is to stop you from fulfilling this feeling of comfort at home? Are you comfortable surrounded by small objects with sentimental value or do you prefer a minimalist, cold and totally rational environment? Are you encouraged by chaos or do you prefer martial order? Do you prefer the industrial esthetic or are you partial to warm and cozy environments? What do you see in the color of the walls? Perhaps, if it does not inspire you, it is time to change it. Don't get obsessed with preconceived ideas about what is right and what is not, but don't lose sight of the internal logic of the objects and the distribution of spaces either. If, for example, your job entails reading for many consecutive hours, you may feel the need to change position frequently to avoid back pains. Getting up periodically to walk around can be a good solution, though you could also use a book rest to enable you to read standing up for a while, something which is a lot more common than you might imagine amongst book editors or writers, for example.

If you are afraid that working from home will make you work more than necessary or if you suspect that you will end up working at night or at weekends, perhaps you should consider the need to radically differentiate the esthetic of your work space from that of the rest of the house. This way you will always be sure which is the work area and which is not, and the appropriate moment for each activity. Setting a strict time limit defining when you must stop working, regardless of the workload can help you discipline yourself and avoid you turning into a workaholic. In this case, close the door when you have finished the working day and forget about it until the next day. If the work space does not take up a separate room, but has, instead, been organized in the corner of a room used for other purposes, such as the dining room for example, perhaps you should try and integrate the esthetic into its environment.

When choosing colors for the walls, it is better to think about light colors that reflect the light rather than dark colors that absorb it. With dark colors you will not have to force your eyes, but they may end up affecting your mood (never your health, which is still believed by some gullible people, influenced by completely false pseudo-scientific studies). There are innumerable science books and reports with more detailed information about the influence of colors on the state of mind, although it still needs to be determined whether this is due mainly to social factors or emotional, purely instinctive, reflexes. It may seem logical that the color red suggests danger because of its association with the color of blood, but it is not that clear why the color white suggests purity - perhaps because of snow, but what happens in tropical countries, then?

On the other hand, and if you are not impressionable, you will probably not be bothered if the color of the walls of your work space is olive green or navy blue, in which case you should probably choose the color in terms of practical or purely esthetic matters, in terms of the color of the furniture or the amount of light you can enjoy, for example.

Do not use too many colored details, instead use them as an elegant element which adds a touch of distinction to a mainly monochromatic deco-

ration. An explosion of color may be appropriate for a child's bedroom, but, as someone once said, "the spectator is distracted by too much color". A good solution for those obsessed with loud colors, but who do not want to go crazy in less than one week, is to paint just one of the room's walls in a striking color, leaving the rest white.

Finally, keep in mind that the light coming from the lamps and spotlights in your work space will affect the color of the walls or, rather, the way you will perceive this color. However you decide to decorate your work area, always remember that all the elements of this space must interact easily, i.e. they must complement each other without causing abrupt breaks, without extravagancies that are not very functional, without details that break the harmony of the whole.

If you achieve a harmonious space thanks to its complete heterodoxy, than do not include a rational piece of furniture without any charm whatsoever. If, on the other hand, you achieve harmony thanks to a certain minimalist spirit, do not be tempted to break it with a spurt of color in the middle of the work space. Also think about the possibility of including a plant, which will turn your work area into a warm, lively and pleasant place. Today's interior designers and architects have generally opted for the elimination of

〈

unnecessary visual barriers. In practice, this means the elimination of those small rooms (used for nothing other than the storage of old junk), tiny windows, long separating corridors and other elements that nobody deems necessary.

Habits have changed as have family structures and the result are open homes which integrate into their surroundings, rather than being separated from them. The aim is to convert all of the rooms in the house into extensions of the exterior – especially if this is a natural environment – rather than turning them into closed and isolated refuges. Hence the boom of lofts, homes with no more than the strictly indispensable walls and houses with huge, almost gigantic windows. Glass walls or sliding doors can be a good option if we want our work space to seem more spacious. If we are lucky enough to live in a house situated in a natural environment and with good views, it would be a sin to enclose and isolate ourselves from the exterior with walls and ridiculously small windows.

Use inconvenient structural elements, such as beams, columns and railings, to help you fulfill innovative and imaginative ideas. Do not try to conceal these elements as you will never succeed in doing so adequately. In fact, it is highly possible that the result of your

efforts will be even more obvious to any casual visitor. Make the most of their virtues and consider them as another part of the furniture, in this case an element with unknown and almost infinite possibilities, paint them, decorate them, use them as a support for some piece of furniture, as a warning panel or as a shelf.

As for paintings, they do not always have to be hung on the wall. Lean them against a ledge and move them when you are tired of them. Do the same with photos or illustrated prints. If you can, place the radiator or heater near your feet or underneath the window so that they heat the air that slips through the cracks, and place the air conditioning device above the door, or far from your head (try to avoid it blowing straight on your head or neck as this will give you a nice cold).

Also think about textiles: carpets, cushions and fabrics for the sofa or chairs. Carpets give warmth... and heat. The same can be said for cushions and any other element covered in leather, a material that is not recommended for hot summers.

Finally, think about the fact that some pieces of furniture, like screens or folding screens for example, can also work as decorative elements.

What should you do if, after working in the same environment for a while, you feel the need for a change? Should all the furniture be changed? Perhaps this is not necessary. The study's decoration can be changed fairly easily and this need not be too expensive. You do not have to change all the furniture or move the desk and cupboards. You will be surprised what you can achieve by just painting the room in a new color and by changing a few select elements. The study can turn into something completely different. If you update the covers of the cushions or sofas, you will get a different look, brighter or more minimalist, depending on your taste. Likewise, if you have decorated your office with photos and frames, you can renew these, as well as some boxes, plant pots, vases. You can also do the same as in your wardrobe and change the decoration of your study according to the seasons. Thus, in the summer you may want to substitute the wool carpets for cotton ones, which are cooler and available in brighter colors, returning to warmer textiles when it turns cold again. Curtains and blinds also allow very visible decorative changes, with little money and without changing the work space too drastically. You are bound to face your job more cheerfully after this renovation.

147

Real examples

Learning from the experience of others

Despite all the ideas and tips presented throughout this book, it is always useful to see examples of how to apply all the theories about organization, distribution and decoration in the work space, to make sure that all the proposals are feasible and seeing the results can serve as a source of inspiration. The following pages will present innovative and original ideas, but most importantly, real ones. Different styles of homes make room for heterogeneous work spaces. The professionals that have moved their study to their home are architects, photographers, musicians, writers, painters and journalists, though they could be any other kind of professional. The spaces have not always been integrated into the home, we will also find annexes especially built to be used as a work area. In some cases, the spaces have been decorated in a minimalist style, while function predominates in others, and we will also find solutions that show a great dose of eclecticism. However, in all cases the personality of the professionals has been reflected in their rooms.

RAVENWOOD HOUSE ▸ David Salmela

This house, property of the National Geographic photographer, Jim Brandenburg, started out as a simple cabin in the woods of Minnesota. Years later, Jim and his wife decided to extend the house with the help of the architect David Salmela, turning it into what it is today: a spectacular home divided into three completely different areas, the details of which, for many, will bring to mind the traditional and elongated Viking mansions. The work space takes up two different levels. The first level is the main study, where Jim has placed a shelf for his books and a rectangular table. Another shelf above the large windows and surrounding the whole room, is for all kinds of photographic material. The second level is for computing materials, such as scanners, computers, printers, etc. This level has an impressive U-shaped table which allows you to move around it without any effort at all, by simply turning the chair or rolling it along with a slight pushing of the feet. A wooden bar serves as a buffer, thus making sure no objects can accidentally fall down to the level below. This space, almost completely built out of cedar wood, has impressive views and huge streams of natural light coming in through the windows in the roof of the house. Some stairs lead to a small upper level, and impressive views can be enjoyed from a small footbridge at the highest point of the house. The views from the first level are equally spectacular. The wood bestows a warm quality on the house, which is perfectly integrated into its environment, the lush woods of Minnesota. To dispense with the windows that surround the whole house, and instead create simple walls, would have been an unforgivable mistake, especially considering we are dealing with a photographer's home. Jim has archived the material used on a daily basis on the upper level of the work space and the material used occasionally on the lower level, thus avoiding having to go up and down the stairs every time he needs to consult a source of information, for example.

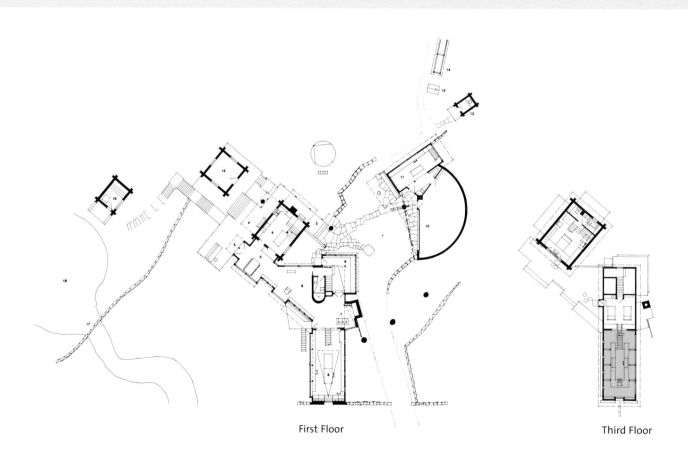

First Floor

Third Floor

JERSEY CITY LOFT ▸ Abelow Connors Sherman Architects

This huge loft in Jersey City, which belongs to a famous musician, was redesigned with the express intention of staying true to its original spirit. In practice, this aspect was translated into an almost completely industrial spirit and the wide variety of materials used in its construction, including exposed brick walls, wooden beams, metal railings, etc. The owner wanted the space to be his home as well as his work study. The work of a music producer involves some very specific needs, such as excellent acoustics, perfect acoustic insulation and, above all, a lot of flexibility. The home and work space with the computing equipment are situated on the bottom level, while the two top floors are reserved for the bedroom and the control and mixing room.

A grand piano and even a regulation height basketball net, gives us an idea of the size of the loft, which dates back to 1880. Some panels can be re-mixed and moved to change the shape and distribution of some of the rooms, easily adapting them to the needs of the owner. A shelf which is several meters long holds the thousands of discs accumulated throughout the owner's professional career and which are regularly used in his job. Without a doubt, the loft has been thought, designed and reformed in terms of its owner's needs, making it really difficult for any other person to feel comfortable in a space with such a specific distribution. In short, its attraction lies in its complete specificity.

First Floor

Second Floor

RENOVATED TOWER › Xavier Gomà

This typical Barcelonese house – called "torres" in Barcelona – from the beginning of the last century, was initially a holiday home for a numerous family. The current owner acquired it in the 1970s and decided to convert it not only into his regular home, but also into his work studio. Thus, he moved the kitchen from the bottom floor where it had always been, to the top floor where it leads directly to an open air terrace, which serves as dining room. This left the bottom floor completely free to be restructured and turned into the owner's study. In this way the top floor can be exclusively dedicated to the home, thus providing more privacy, and the work areas can be totally differentiated from those dedicated to everyday life. In general, the distribution of the house was respected, though some walls were eliminated in order to gain space. The work area, which takes up several rooms (two of them connected by an arch), has been thought out and distributed in a totally functional way: wooden floors, large and clear tables, tables placed as close as possible to the windows, direct access to a private patio, raised shelves for filing material and small drawers and cupboards for less used material... The space is not only practical, but also elegant and attractive, thanks to the combination of esthetically classic elements, such as those doors and windows with mosaic glass, with other completely contemporary elements, like some of the chairs that can be seen in the photos. A chest of drawers with narrow and very long drawers, especially for plans, dominates the central space of one of the rooms and breaks the mould of that annoying tendency to always place filing cabinets against the wall.

APARTMENT ON MICHIGAN AVENUE ▸ Pablo Uribe

It is not necessary to have a huge work space to be able to work comfortably. This small studio in Miami Beach, which belongs to Pablo Uribe, the architect who also designed it, proves this point. Situated on the second floor of a building from 1951, it barely has one room, bathroom, kitchen and studio, all integrated into one space. Basically, its attraction lies in its simplicity. Pablo Uribe did not need to store large amounts of material, so he opted for a discreet and almost minimalist solution, with great personality. The first thing the owner did was to restore some of the elements that fit the 1950s esthetic, the period in which the dwelling was built, such as the aluminum windows. The wooden floor was painted in white to add a contemporary touch to the studio and make it visually bigger. The small work space simply consists of a table and a transparent plastic chair and a translucent plastic chest of drawers. The table and chair are practically invisible, which increases the feeling of space, a surprising effect if we think about how miniscule the studio really is. Pablo works with the bare minimum of elements: the computer is a laptop, which means he has not had to find a space for those inconvenient and annoying towers that come with desktop computers. In fact, even the computer's peripherals (the speakers, for example) are transparent. The few books that Pablo may need in his job on a daily basis have been placed on the floor in a well-lit corner to the left of the window. This corner has been especially fitted out for reading, with a chair that sits next to an auxiliary desk with a flexible lamp. Although the studio, and the work space especially, has a considerable amount of natural light, Pablo has opted to add an extra lamp to his work table. In a studio designed with such care and attention to detail (even the television is white), the bed and couple of dark wooden chairs add a touch of elegance. This detail which subtly breaks the monochromatic whole, is what gives the studio a captivating personality.

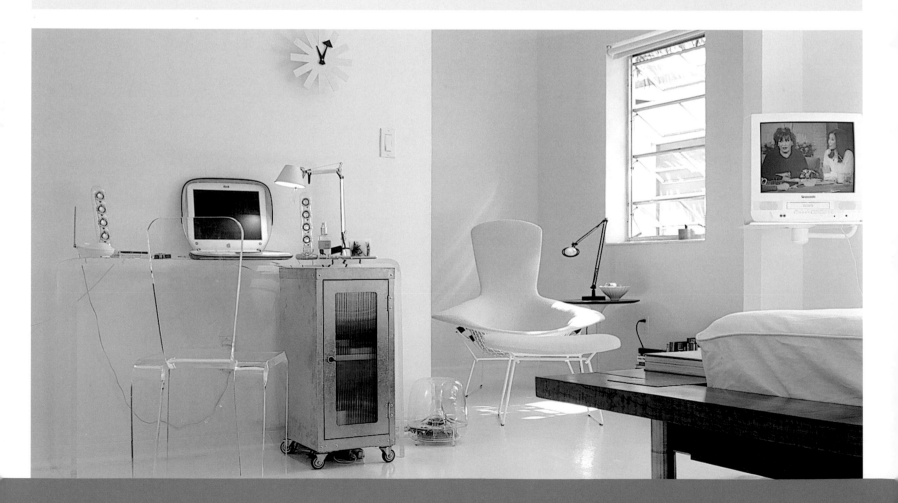

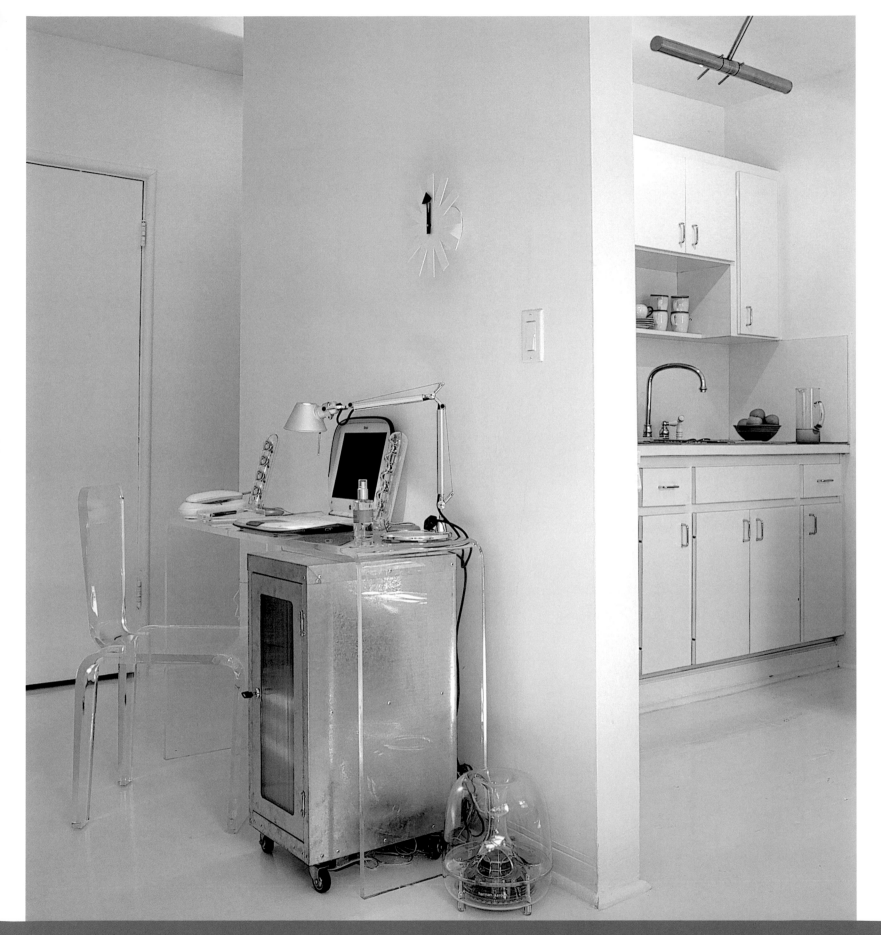

169

PAINTER AND ARCHITECT ▸ Elizabeth Alford

This New York space has been created to work as a home and work area to accommodate the two jobs of its owner, the painter and architect Elizabeth Alford. A shelf on which Alford has placed dozens of jars of sand, which she uses for her paintings – a kind of decorative element in itself – serves as a border and marks the separation between the space dedicated to the home and the one dedicated to work. The wooden panels unite the walls and ceiling with the floor, thus giving the work area a completely uniform visual style. An intelligent distribution of the lights, like the fluorescent one that crosses the space from one end to the other, adds warmth to the work area and perfectly solves the problem of lack of natural light. The project's excellent result, designed by Elizabeth Alford herself, is partly thanks to the extraordinary palette of colors in which not one single element breaks the harmony of the whole. Elizabeth Alford has placed the computers and printer that she uses for her job as an architect on a long table made of metal elements and the same kind of wood that covers the walls and ceiling. Behind this is a filing cabinet where she keeps the material she uses every day. Almost hidden behind the wooden panel is a small corner with another, smaller table, some shelves and a chest of drawers for plans, as well as a book rest to be able to read while standing. The majority of the books that the owner uses in her job have been placed on a piece of furniture in the entrance of the space, in front of a small table with four chairs. The exceptional nature of this space lies, without a doubt, in the almost incredible harmony of all the elements that make up the space, thought out and selected with the smallest detail in mind.

APARTMENT ON ROSOMAN STREET ► Felicity Bell

As the rest of the projects in this chapter, this small apartment in the Clerkenwell neighborhood of London doubles as a home and work study. The first thing that strikes you is the extraordinary amount of natural light coming in through four huge windows which reach the ceiling and perfectly illuminate every last corner of the work area and bedroom. An imaginary line divides the apartment into two clearly differentiated parts. The first corresponds to the couple's bedroom and bathroom – the place is owned by Felicity Bell (who was in charge of the renovation) and Christian Papa. The second area is the work space, which also doubles as a dining room. This room has a round table, some furniture and low shelves with several magazines and books. The kitchen is situated against the lateral wall and has been designed in the same minimalist style as the rest of the house. At the other extreme, in a corner, is one of the apartment's greatest attractions: a work space that can be hidden by pulling a folding screen. This is where the owners have placed the computer, several shelves for filing

material and even a large drawing easel. When the screen is closed, the space serves as a dining and living room. When it is opened, the space takes on a completely different appearance and turns into a work studio where it is also possible to receive clients, thanks to its special distribution. The rather neutral decoration, in which the building's industrial character has hardly intervened, helps make visitors feel that they are not having a meeting in the private dining room of this couple of architects. And, similarly, when the folding screen is closed to hide the work space behind it, the couple can completely forget about work and can eat and watch television without feeling they are doing so in their office. Another sliding door separates the entrance area (which turns into an entrance hall) with a double personality. The color white of the majority of the furniture, walls and windows (which take up a good part of the exterior walls) helps give the space maximum luminosity and a feeling of space, and a pure esthetic, despite the apartment's smallness.

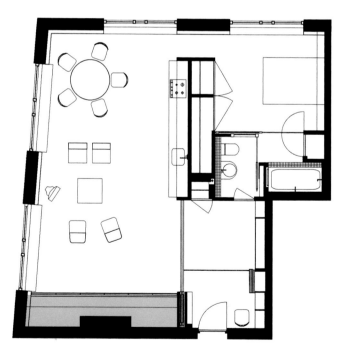

Plan

SIEGEL-SWANSEA LOFT ▸ Abelow Connors Sherman Architects

The writer Joel Siegel and his wife, the painter Ena Swansea, decided to renovate this early 20th century New York loft to turn it into their home and work space. Both agreed to respect most of the details revealing the loft's industrial past, such as the pipes, some ventilation shafts and even the electrical installation and the arched ceiling. The floor, however, has been completely renovated, except in the central room – the work space – where some original wooden strips can still be seen. This medium-sized office is situated in the center of the loft, which makes it something like an island decorated in a completely different way to the rest of the home. The office also serves as a place where one can relax and listen to music in a warm and cozy environment. Apparently difficult to combine and harmonize esthetics, such as the industrial elements mentioned before and the owner's, Ena Swansea, own paintings, have successfully integrated in this loft. In the work space, the color white, dominant throughout this loft, turns into warm colors and lighting of slightly ochre tones. The furniture of this office/studio also contrasts strongly with the rest of the loft. If white and minimalist furniture generally predominates in the home area, the office furniture is made of wood and rather classical. A small shelf above the desk allows dozens of CDs to be stored and to be within easy reach, while a huge shelf which takes up the whole wall holds literally hundreds of books and filing material. A small piece of furniture next to the table serves as an auxiliary multi-purpose shelf (in this case, the owners have chosen to use it for the music system and some more CDs). The bedrooms and bathrooms have been distributed throughout the loft, while a large room opposite the apartment's entrance – well-lit, thanks to huge windows – serves as a space to paint paintings of gigantic dimensions.

Plan

ROSENBERG RESIDENCE ▸ Belmont Freeman Architects

This home in New York's Lower Manhattan is divided into two almost equal spaces (so, really this is a duplex) and is situated inside a former commercial building which dates back to the beginning of the 20th century. The first, lower, space is the one dedicated to the home. Here we can find a dining or living room of considerable dimensions, and a kitchen and two bedrooms with en-suite bathrooms. This part of the home, very well illuminated (the building is on a corner and receives plenty of natural light), was renovated to be used as a residence in the 1980s. The second space is devoted to the work studio. As seen in the photos, the floor of the work areas is cement, while the floor on the lower level, of the home, is wood. This helps to distinguish the two areas and give them their own personality, one more industrial and the other warm and more cozy. In fact, one of the main problems the architects were faced with when redesigning the home, was how to visually and stylistically differentiate the two spaces while integrating them at the same time. They achieved this with an ingenious use of materials and by playing with the gray of the cement and the brown of the wood (notice the elements that are of wood on one level and of cement or gray on the next, and vice versa, resulting in a global view similar to the parallel rows of a chess board). The home's two levels are connected by a staircase similar to that found on boats. It was not necessary to build a staircase, simply to open a flap door in the floor of the upper level. Two screens, one of transparent glass and another of plaster, can be easily moved to reorganize the space according to the owner's taste. The work space is almost minimalist, spartan. A small table with a chair and a desk lamp, accompanied by a chest of drawers, is all that the owner, an art lover, needs to work. In a cupboard behind him, he can easily store all the necessary material and the windows to his right, as well as the lights in the ceiling, give him plenty of light to read and work without any problem whatsoever.

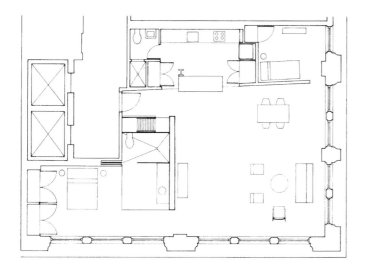

First Floor

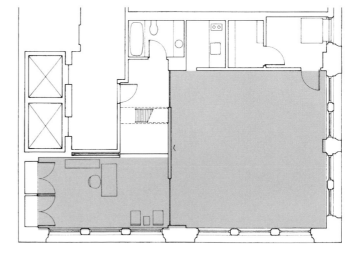

Second Floor

PAINTING STUDIO ► Dan Schimmel

This former textile factory situated in the old industrial neighborhood of Philadelphia has been reformed by its owner, the artist Dan Schimmel (also the director of a nonprofit art gallery), with the aim of turning it into his home and workshop. The result is eclectic, like Dan's tastes. He hasn't followed a preconceived plan to decorate the space, rather he put together the accumulated objects picked up from the street with pieces of furniture of different materials, fabrics, cushions and curtains of different origins and, of course, paintings of completely opposing esthetics. In fact, some of the old industrial elements of the space have been easily restructured for domestic use, while others originally meant for use in part of the home have been reused as part of the furniture in the work area. For example, a large table formerly used as a table to cut the patterns of the fabrics, is now a desk on which Dan has places his computer and computing material. In the

kitchen, a similar table serves as a work space... for cooking. Some lights and lamps which were originally going to be discarded later, were used to illuminate certain parts of the loft which were left in the dark. The result is, to say the least, odd: an amalgam of anti-ethical esthetic objects without any order or coordination, which, however, end up achieving a kind of harmony of their own, far from any conventionalism, though the end result is not too unorthodox so as to provoke rejection. Dan chose the space, which is flooded with natural light and has spectacular views of the city, for its spaciousness. The workshop where Dan paints his works is separated from the space used as a home by a wall about 5 ft. high. The owner added windows from old houses to this wall to fill the hole between the end of the wall and the ceiling, which allows light to enter and at the same time makes for a radical, yet subtle, division of the spaces.

Photographers

Companies